A Soul's Purpose

To know thyself through biblical principles and scientific facts, a guide for good health, healing, positive change and manifesting.

Carmel Fleming

with Tamela Barras

Dedication

To my beloved mother-

for choosing sacrifice over comfort,
for building a better life for your children,
for holding us together when letting go would
have been easier,
and for loving us faithfully to your final breath.

You left this world when I was ten,
but you have never left my life.

You live in the strength you planted in me,
and in the love I carry forward.

-Carmel

Introduction

My story begins with loss. As a young boy, I lost my mother, and with her passing, a deep emptiness took root in my soul. That wound shaped my life in ways I didn't understand at the time. In my search to numb the pain, I turned to drugs and destructive choices that carried me far from the man God created me to be.

Years passed, and the distance from God expanded. One night, I found myself standing in a small, rundown kitchen — a place that reflected the condition of my heart. In my mind, life was under control, yet I was walking through a dark valley I could not see clearly. It was there, in that quiet despair, that God appeared.

I heard a voice ask me, "Do you believe in God?" The question came again, firm and undeniable: "Do you believe in God?"

Then it spoke: "If you believe in God, fall on your knees and worship Him."

With trembling, I dropped to the floor. In that moment, I felt the presence of Jesus so near that I found myself at His feet, so present I could feel His sandals. I had what I can only describe as a personal visitation from God.

Then came the words that changed my life forever: "There is nothing in the world worth losing your soul for. Tell everyone."

As His peace washed over me, I wept, wrapped in the fullness of His love—yet in the same breath, I sensed the weight of eternity, both its glory and its sorrow. I could hear the chaos of hell, feel the despair of separation from God, and sense the emptiness that waits for those who live without Him. That moment made everything clear: only in Him is there life; without Him, there is only death.

From that night forward, my calling was solidified. God saved me to live differently and to tell others about Him.

This book, A Soul's Purpose, is the fruit of that calling. It contains the truths God has taught me through His Word, through years of walking with Him, and through the salvation of my own life.

But this book is not mine alone. My daughter and I wrote it together. In the process, we discovered not only the depth of God's truth, but also the gift of each other. Writing this book side by side drew us closer as father and daughter, and more importantly, closer to God Himself. What began as my life's work became our shared work, a testimony of faith, family, and the unshakable love of God.

My prayer is that as you read these pages, you won't just see my story. You'll hear God's voice calling you, reminding you — as He reminded me — that nothing in this world is worth your soul.

This is my testimony. This is my soul's purpose. And now, it becomes yours to carry, too.

Carmel Fleming

Chapter 1: The Soul of Man

Explore and experience with us the soul of man—its nature and its divine relationship to the mind, body, soul and spirit. What makes us human? What makes us sacred? Are we simply the result of biological evolution, or are we something more?

Some say we evolved from apes through a chain of physical transformations. Others believe we were placed into existence by divine intent. Both views attempt to make sense of our origin, but there is a spiritual distinction inserted into the center of our DNA—something that sets us apart. We are more than flesh and blood. We are vessels of divine essence. We are spiritual beings having a human experience.

The Bible says in Genesis 1:26, "Let us make man in our image, in our likeness." And in Genesis 2:7, "The Lord God formed the man from the dust of the ground and breathed into his nostrils the breath of life, and man became a living soul."

The concept of being made in God's image is not about physical form. It is about spiritual capacity. It is about divine characteristics embedded within us: the ability to reason, to create, to love, to forgive, to lead, and to connect. These qualities reflect God's essence in a form we can barely comprehend. They form the architecture of the soul.

Imagine the journey before birth. Picture a realm beyond time, beyond stars and matter, where unborn souls drifted in a river of vibration, swimming in the frequency of pure love. Do you remember it?

Bliss surrounded you—not the fleeting happiness we chase on Earth, but an unshakable state of joy and peace that needed no explanation. In that place, you were whole. You didn't have to perform, to prove, to achieve. You just were. Safe. Seen. Loved. Aligned.

We yearned: to touch, to taste, to see, to feel. To walk the Earth, to love, to learn. You longed to enter this world. You knew the cost—that there would be heartbreak, betrayal, fear, sickness, and even death. But you said yes.

This is the soul's boldness—the divine courage to descend into form.

And so began the miracle. Life started with a race—not a random scramble, but a sacred competition. When the sperm is released, it enters a hostile environment. Few survive. But you—you endured. You navigated layers of resistance and unknown territory. The first to arrive does not fertilize the egg. It's not about speed alone. It's about endurance. Strength. Direction. You were chosen.

The moment of conception was biology and it was a divine appointment. The Creator set into motion a sequence of life, and through infinite possibilities—you became.

You were woven together with intent. You were knit in your mother's womb with divine craftsmanship. Psalm 139:14 reminds us: "I praise you, for I am fearfully and wonderfully made."

Then came awareness. At a certain age, you became conscious of self. You recognized that you were more than a body. You had thoughts, emotions, and longings. You became aware of your place in the world. And with that awareness came questions:

Why am I here? What is my purpose? What does my life mean?

Do you remember your first memory? Was it a warm one—your mother's touch, your father's laugh, a sunbeam on your face? Or was it a darker recollection—war, loss, fear, hunger? Either way, that memory became a part of your soul's tapestry.

You came through the stars to survive and to become. Every moment of your journey—every joy, every trauma, every lesson—has brought you to this moment. And this moment, right now, is all that matters.

The soul is eternal. It is your truest self—unchanging, unwavering. The mind changes. The body fades. But the soul remains. It is the spark of God within you, a living thread that ties you to the divine.

You are purposely designed to live in this universe. You are not a random collection of atoms floating without direction. You are a divine being, created to reflect God's light, truth, and love.

And so we say: find your purpose. Become aligned. Let your soul rise to meet your spirit. Let your body become a temple that houses something holy. Let your mind become clear, free from deception and illusion.

You were created to vibrate, to add flavor and light to the world. You were made to evolve, biologically and spiritually. You are the next step in a divine story.

You are human. You are divine. And your soul knows the way home.

Chapter 2: To Know Thyself

Hebrews 4:12 reminds us: "The word of God is living and active, sharper than any two-edged sword, piercing to the division of soul and spirit, of joints and marrow; it judges the thoughts and attitudes of the heart." This sacred verse is more than poetry; it is revelation. It speaks of the word as a divine instrument that knows the intricacies of our being—discerning where the soul ends and the spirit begins. Only the divine can truly separate what is so deeply intertwined.

The soul is the "I am" in man. It is the actor and the spectator—the one who feels and the one who observes. It carries the memories and the whispers of eternity. It is complex, supernatural, and profoundly sacred. The soul is the interface between heaven and Earth, spirit and matter. It is a belief that we are more than flesh and blood. We are cosmic beings, infused with divine intention, and far more powerful than we dare to imagine.

Science affirms this truth. In quantum mechanics, particles behave differently depending on whether they're being observed. This phenomenon, known as the observer effect, suggests that the presence of consciousness can alter physical reality. In medicine, the placebo effect shows us how belief can shift biology—where simply believing something works can make it so. This is no small thing. This is sacred design.

To know thyself, is to begin to understand the power of your own being. We are co-creators in the divine dance of life.

We are known by our fruit. Galatians 5:22-23 teaches that the fruit of the Spirit is love, joy, and peace. These are the attributes of the spirit: kindness, goodness, faithfulness, gentleness, and self-control. These fruit are the evidence of a soul aligning with its Creator. In contrast, when we live from fear, hate, judgment, and pride, we operate from a fractured self, disconnected from our Source.

Proverbs 23:7 states, "As a man thinks in his heart, so is he." Your inner thoughts become your reality. It's what you think, it's what you say, and what you do. What you truly believe in your heart—that is what shapes your life. Your thoughts become emotions. Your emotions become behaviors. Your behaviors become reality.

If you believe that you are broken, you will behave as though you are. If you believe you are whole, you will carry yourself as such. Believe you are loved by God, you can walk in authority.

Your heart is your internal compass. It is the seat of your desires, your convictions, and your faith. If your heart is poisoned by deceit, bitterness, or shame, your journey will be steep. But if your heart is filled with integrity, gratitude, and grace, you will rise. The truth is, you become the person you believe yourself to be.

Luke 8:17 warns us, "For nothing is hidden that will not be made known, nor is anything secret that will not come to light." The secrets we bury—the self-deceptions, the unspoken regrets, the sins we rationalize—they all rise eventually. Either in this life, or before the Creator Himself. There is no hiding from the Light.

We must stop justifying what we know is wrong. Grace is not a license for rebellion. Yes, the debt of sin has been paid. Yes, we are saved by grace, not by works. But to know yourself is to walk in the light, because God is light, and in Him there is no darkness (1 John 1:5).

To walk in the light is to live honestly. Humbly. Transparently. It doesn't mean perfection, but it does require sincerity. We confess. We repent. We try again. We grow. We become.

And in this becoming, we must learn to give from joy. 2 Corinthians 9:7 reminds us, "Each one must give as he has decided in his heart, not reluctantly or under compulsion, for God loves a cheerful giver." Whether it is love, service, energy, or time—give freely or do not give at all. The heart matters more than the hand.

If you want to walk in freedom, you must also walk in truth. Do not let fear whisper lies to your soul. Speak life. Speak grace. Speak identity. Tell yourself who you are, and then become it.

If you say, "I will change," then act on it. If you say, "I will be healthy," then nourish your body. If you say, "I will grow spiritually," then seek God with intention. Your actions must mirror your declarations. Otherwise, you begin to doubt your own voice. And once you stop trusting yourself, your faith will falter.

A liar can lead—but only into darkness, even when that liar is you. True leadership begins with truth. That's why integrity must start within. It's not just a public virtue; it's a personal one. Be someone your own soul can trust.

Keep the promises you make to your soul. This is how confidence is built. This is how alignment is restored. This is how healing begins.

You do not need to be perfect. You need only be honest. With God. With others. With yourself.

To know thyself is to walk with the Creator. To walk with the Creator is to live in the light. And where the light is, there is clarity. There is power. And above all—there is freedom.

Reflection Practice:

Meditation Prompt: Ask yourself: "What lies have I told myself?" Sit with it. Do not judge. Just listen. Let the truth arise.

Journal Exercise: Write a letter to your younger self. Tell them what you've learned. Tell them what you now know to be true.

Affirmation:

I walk in truth. I am whole. I am a soul made in divine image. I am trustworthy. I keep my word to myself and to my Creator.

Chapter 3: Good Master

The story of the rich young ruler (Matthew 19:16–26) is not simply a lesson in obedience or wealth—it is a mirror for the soul. It's a powerful lesson on self-deception and the condition of the heart. A young man, wealthy and eager, approached Yeshua (Jesus) and asked, "Good Master, what must I do to inherit eternal life?"

With wisdom, Yeshua responded, "Why do you call Me good? There is no one good but God. But if you desire eternal life, keep the commandments." Yeshua named those that pertain to how we treat others—honor your father and mother, do not murder, do not steal, do not lie, love your neighbor as yourself.

The young man replied confidently, "All these I have kept since my youth." He believed he was blameless. But Yeshua saw his heart. He said, "One thing you lack. Go, sell all you have, give to the poor, and you will have treasure in heaven. Then come, follow Me."

The young man went away sorrowful. Not because the request was unclear, but because his heart was already given to his riches. He wanted the kingdom, but he didn't want to give up his riches. His identity was too tangled in his possessions.

This story is an invitation to look inward.

What are you unwilling to let go of? What do you trust more than God?

The young ruler was morally upright, religiously devout, and socially admired. But eternal life is not inherited through performance or appearances. It is birthed through surrender.

Yeshua wasn't condemning wealth. He was confronting idolatry. The heart of the Gospel is this: You can do everything right on the outside and still miss the truth on the inside.

God doesn't need your perfection. He desires your devotion. He desires your heart. True spiritual transformation begins when we open our clenched fists and release the things we grasp too tightly—be it money, pride, image, comfort, or control.

Wealth is not evil. It is a tool. But when it becomes a treasure, it can become a trap. True prosperity is wholeness—a life marked by peace, wisdom, health, and alignment with God.

Scripture says, "The blessing of the Lord makes rich, and He adds no sorrow with it" (Proverbs 10:22). This means Godly abundance does not drain your soul; it nourishes it. When our hearts are surrendered, even wealth becomes a way to serve.

Yet we must be watchful.

Poverty is a thief that robs dignity, opportunity, and life itself. Millions of children die each year from its grasp. But wealth, when idolized or hoarded, becomes a silent killer too—eroding compassion, clarity, and dependence on God.

The commandments were never meant to be a checklist. They are mirrors revealing the health of our souls. Yeshua used them not to validate the young man's righteousness, but to expose his blind spot.

We each have them—blind spots we protect, comforts we justify, patterns we excuse. But the spiritual life requires accountability.

God has done His part. Now we must rise. Each day is a gift, a sacred window to choose again. To begin again. Consciousness is your spiritual steering wheel. Use it wisely.

Choose your thoughts. Direct your emotions. Speak with purpose. Every word and action is a seed. And the seed you plant is the seed that will grow. What are you planting?

Be mindful of your inner soil. Bitterness, pride, fear—they grow weeds. But gratitude, humility, and truth prepare you to bloom.

James 4:6 says, "God resists the proud but gives grace to the humble."

Humility is not weakness. It is power under surrender. It is the spiritual posture that invites grace and unlocks destiny. It is the soil in which your purpose can grow.

Spiritual principles do not respond to force. They respond to truth. They respond to love. They respond to consistency.

Gratitude is not simply a virtue; it is a spiritual strategy. It recalibrates your energy, your perspective, and your chemistry. Scientists have found that gratitude increases dopamine and serotonin—the brain's feel-good chemicals.

Harvard Health Publishing states: "Gratitude helps people feel more positive emotions, relish good experiences, improve their health, deal with adversity, and build strong relationships."

Be grateful for the small things, as a thankful heart invites miracles. A humble spirit welcomes wisdom. A conscious mind builds a legacy.

10 Ways to Practice Gratitude

Start and End with Thanks – Greet the day and close it in thanksgiving.

Gratitude Journal – Write 3-5 things daily you're thankful for.

Reframe Challenges – Ask, "What is this teaching me?"

Observe Nature – Let the Earth remind you of God's faithfulness.

Serve Others – Give, and your joy will multiply.

Speak It Out Loud – Declare, "Thank You, God!" daily.

Meditate on Scripture – Anchor your soul in truth.

Reflect on Your Journey – Remember how far you've come.

Practice Stillness – Let silence reveal gratitude within.

Surround Yourself with Gratitude – Be with those who see the good.

Let go of what no longer serves you. Like the rich young ruler, you are invited to follow the Master. But first, examine your heart. What are you clinging to?

Whatever you release, God can multiply. Whatever you surrender, He can sanctify. Let this be the chapter where you choose truth over comfort, purpose over possessions, and transformation over appearance.

Eternal life is not far. It begins the moment you say yes.

Reflection Practice:

Meditation Prompt: Ask: "God, what do I treasure more than You?" Sit quietly and the answer will present itself (maybe not in this meditation session but the revelation will come).

Journal Exercise: Write about a time you felt torn between God and something else. What did you choose? What did you learn?

Affirmation:

I choose surrender. I walk in truth. I am grateful. I am guided. My heart belongs to God.

Chapter 4: Spiritual Bonds

Many of us walk through life unaware of the invisible cords we carry—spiritual bonds that link us to past relationships, traumas, agreements, and versions of ourselves that no longer serve who we are becoming. A spiritual bond is more than an emotional memory. It is a spiritual connection that can nourish or drain you, elevate or entangle you. To step fully into your divine purpose, you must first make peace with your past.

Spiritual bonds form when your spirit becomes deeply bonded to another person, experience, or belief system. These connections can happen in relationships, both romantic and platonic; through trauma and loss; or through repeated habits and patterns. When these ties are godly, they bring life. When they are unhealthy or ungodly, they will stagnate you.

Scripture shows us examples of godly spiritual bonds—David and Jonathan had a bond rooted in brotherly love and loyalty (1 Samuel 18:1). But the Bible also warns of bonds that lead us away from God. Proverbs 5:22 says, "The evil deeds of the wicked ensnare them; the cords of their sins hold them fast."

Ask yourself:

Who or what am I still tied to?

What version of myself am I afraid to let go of?

How has my comfort contributed to ungodly spiritual bonds?

Have I made peace with my past, or am I still carrying the weight of it?

To break a spiritual bond is not to erase a memory. It is to untangle the emotional and spiritual influence that memory has on your present. It is to reclaim your power from what you once gave it to. This is a process of grief, grace, and growth.

Forgiveness is key. Forgive yourself. Forgive others. Not because they deserve it, but because you deserve peace. Release the bitterness. Let go of the control. Ask God to cut every spiritual cord that no longer aligns with His purpose for your life.

Speak this prayer:

"God, I release every unhealthy soul tie and agreement I made in pain, fear, or ignorance. I reclaim my spirit. I forgive those who hurt me, and I forgive myself. Heal the wounds. Restore what was broken. And align me with your purpose for my life. Amen."

Wounds left unhealed become triggers. And triggers control behavior. You cannot walk into your divine calling while still bleeding from past battles. Healing is not forgetting. It is remembering without reliving. It is seeing the scar and recognizing your survival.

Jesus said in John 10:10, "I have come that they may have life, and have it more abundantly." You are not meant to live half-alive, stuck in sorrow, guilt, or regret. You are meant to live whole.

Begin with honesty. Be honest about what hurt you. Be honest about how you coped. Then bring those truths before God. Invite Him into your story. Healing is often slow, layered, and sacred. But it is always possible.

Once you begin to release negative influence, you begin to remember who you are. Your river of purpose will begin to flow into the flavor you bring to this life—your presence, your gift, your light.

Romans 8:28 reminds us, "And we know that in all things God works for the good of those who love Him, who have been called according to His purpose."

Purpose is not always revealed in a flash. Sometimes it unfolds slowly. Sometimes it is discovered through pain. But it always begins with alignment. When your soul aligns with your spirit, and your spirit aligns with God, you begin to flow with ease.

Progress begins with a thought, then a step. Use what you have. Start where you are. The time is now. Every moment has prepared you for this one. Move forward. Trust the process.

Chapter 5: The Power of Encouragement

Encouragement is not a soft word. It is a compliment and a polite pat on the back. Encouragement is a spiritual force—a divine fuel that ignites possibility, resurrects hope, and breathes new life into weary bones. It is the antidote to despair, the medicine for a heart that feels forgotten.

To encourage someone is to transfer courage into them. It is to speak life when life feels silent. It is to remind them of who they are when they can no longer see it. It is to reflect their greatness when all they can see is failure.

The Scriptures are full of encouragement:

"Therefore encourage one another and build each other up, just as in fact you are doing." —1 Thessalonians 5:11

"Anxiety weighs down the heart, but a kind word cheers it up." —Proverbs 12:25

Encouragement uplifts. It restores. It heals. It creates space for growth. And it costs us very little.

Some are called to preach. Others may be called to write books or lead movements. But every believer is called to encourage. Encouragement is holy work. It is a divine assignment to be a light in someone else's darkness.

When someone stands on the edge of giving up, your words can be the bridge that carries them back to hope. When someone doubts their value, your words can be a mirror that reflects their worth.

Encouragement can be flattery or shallow praise but most importantly it is rooted in truth. It acknowledges both struggle and strength. It recognizes the truth of what is—and still holds on to the hope of what can be.

Words carry weight. They are vessels of spirit. Scripture reminds us that "Death and life are in the power of the tongue" (Proverbs 18:21).

To encourage is to breathe life.

How to Encourage Others

Correct in Love — Speak truth, but wrap it in grace. Correction is a form of love when it is done with humility, respect, and the aim to build.

Celebrate Small Steps — Not every mountain must be moved in a day. Acknowledge growth, even if it seems minor. People blossom with belief.

Don't Compare — Comparison diminishes confidence, but timely encouragement can restore it, speak life into others when the opportunity presents itself and their hearts are open to receive it.

Ask Before Advising — Sometimes people need to be heard before they are helped. Ask, "Is there something I can do to help you or do you need someone to listen?"

Be Present — You don't need all the right words. Being with someone in their pain speaks volumes.

Encouragement is honest. It is about acknowledging the reality of pain and still believing in the possibility of healing. It says, "Yes, this is hard. But you are not alone." It's the language of elevation. It lifts the atmosphere. It raises the vibration of a room. It draws people out of isolation and into community.

When you choose to elevate others, you elevate yourself. You rise with every soul you uplift. This world needs more lifters. Let your words and deeds be a ladder. Let your voice be a light. Let your presence be a reminder: we were never meant to walk this path alone.

When we speak words of encouragement, we plant seeds of belief. We create space for new outcomes. We call into existence things not seen. Sometimes, the only difference between failure and breakthrough is one word of encouragement spoken at the right time.

We don't know the battles people are fighting. But we do know that everyone is in need of hope. Everyone is strengthened by sincere, Spirit-led encouragement. You elevate by building someone else up.

When David was distressed, Scripture says he "encouraged himself in the Lord his God" (1 Samuel 30:6). There will be times when no one else sees your struggle. When that day comes, self-encouragement will be necessary.

Speak to your soul:

"Why, my soul, are you downcast? Put your hope in God, for I will yet praise Him." (Psalm 42:11)

Pray over yourself. Affirm the promises of God. Declare truth over your situation. Needing encouragement is not a sign of weakness. There is wisdom in seeking it.

Reflection Practice:

Encouragement List: Write down the names of five people you can encourage this week. Send them a message, a prayer, a kind word.

Journal Prompt: What encouraging words do you need to hear today? Write them to yourself in a note.

Encouragement Awareness: Reflect on times you may have intentionally encouraged someone. What did you say that elevated them?

Affirmation:

I am a vessel of encouragement. My words heal, uplift, and inspire. I receive courage, and I give courage. I guard my tongue, and I choose to elevate.

Chapter 6: The Power of a Focused Mind

"A double-minded man is unstable in all his ways."
—James 1:8

To be double-minded is to live in conflict. It is to be split down the middle—half in faith, half in fear. It is like trying to build a house on shifting sand. Nothing can stand firm where there is no foundation. A double-minded life is filled with hesitation, procrastination, and confusion. It is the internal tug-of-war between who you are and who you were, between what God has called you to and what the world tries to convince you to be.

The double-minded person is not necessarily evil or lazy. More often, they are overwhelmed. They are trying to walk in two directions at once, trying to serve two masters. They want purpose, but they also want comfort. They want to grow, but they resist the discomfort growth requires.

Procrastination is the fruit of the doubleminded. We delay what we fear. And we fear what we do not believe we can control. Fear, born of doubt, is the thief of time and progress.

Focus, however, is the remedy. It is the sacred discipline of intention. Focus cuts through fear like light through darkness. When you set your heart and mind on a single purpose—anchored in faith—you begin to move with clarity and power.

The mind is a spiritual gateway. Thoughts are not neutral. Every thought builds something—peace or anxiety, love or bitterness, progress or paralysis. This is why we are instructed to renew our minds daily, to take every thought and make it obedient to Christ (Romans 12:2, 2 Corinthians 10:5).

You are a spiritual architect. Every moment, you are either constructing a temple or tearing one down. The words you speak, the emotions you allow, the thoughts you nurture—all of it matters. Your life is built from the inside out.

"For our struggle is not against flesh and blood, but against the rulers, against the authorities, against the powers of this dark world, and against the spiritual forces of evil in the heavenly realms." —Ephesians 6:12

This is a spiritual war, and it's waged daily over your focus, your energy, your joy, and your identity. That is why clarity and discipline are non-negotiable. You must train your spirit to recognize distractions dressed as opportunity. You must guard your gates—your ears, your eyes, your heart. Not everything deserves access to your energy.

Do not entertain energies, people, or ideas that you do not understand. Do not dabble in the occult, witchcraft, or spiritual practices that open portals to confusion and destruction. These things are harmful. They are spiritual viruses that infect your discernment, dull your focus, and separate you from divine alignment.

We live in a world that glorifies chaos. But God honors devotion.

When focus is disciplined and channeled properly, it becomes a supernatural force. It develops spiritual authority. It builds mental endurance. It sharpens discernment.

Focus breaks cycles. Focus opens doors. Focus is the foundation for discipline.

When your focus is rooted in your God-given purpose, everything around you begins to shift. You begin to see with new eyes. You begin to hear what others miss. You begin to walk with confidence because you know where you are going and who is going with you.

Jesus said, "The eye is the lamp of the body. If your eyes are good, your whole body will be full of light. But if your eyes are bad your whole body will be full of darkness." (Matthew 6:22). A focused vision fills your life with light, clarity, and power but a scattered mind is fertile ground for confusion. A focused mind becomes the resting place of wisdom.

Ways to begin cultivating focus:

Start With Solitude and Stillness — Begin each day with quiet. Breathe deeply. Align with God's spirit. Invite God to direct your thoughts.

Pray for Discernment — Ask God to help you distinguish distractions from divine assignments.

Write Your Vision — Habakkuk 2:2 says, "Write the vision and make it plain." A clear vision keeps your mind anchored.

Practice Daily Disciplines — Focus is like a muscle. It strengthens with repetition. Set time each day for reading, reflection, and focused work.

Declutter Your Environment — Your outer world reflects your inner world. Create spaces that support your purpose.

Fast from Noise — Take breaks from social media, news, and overstimulation. Silence is sacred. It resets your spiritual ears.

Surround Yourself with Focused People — Iron sharpens iron. Walk with those who sharpen your focus.

Affirmation:

I am focused. I am clear. I serve one master. I serve the One true God with my whole heart, my whole mind, and my whole strength. My focus creates flow. My flow creates fruit. My fruit glorifies God.

Focus is a lifestyle. It is the posture of the disciplined believer. It is the lens through which success is bread. Be rooted. Be sharp. Be single-minded. Because when your mind is aligned with your purpose, and your purpose is aligned with God, you become unstoppable.

Chapter 7: Sacred Order

Order is not a suggestion—it is a divine principle. From the alignment of the stars in the sky to the precision of the heartbeat within your chest, the universe was not created randomly. God is a God of order. In His presence, everything flows with purpose. There is harmony in His design, rhythm in His intentions, and clarity in His voice.

"For God is not the author of confusion but of peace, as in all the churches of the saints." —1 Corinthians 14:33

This is why Scripture instructs us:

"Let all things be done decently and in order." —1 Corinthians 14:40

When your life is in disorder, it creates internal noise. That noise distorts your perception and clouds your spiritual discernment. You may feel anxious, unmotivated, disoriented because disorder muffles your ability to hear Him.

When you bring order into your space, you make room for God to dwell there. A clean home, a structured day, a focused mind—these are not small matters. They are acts of spiritual reverence. They signal to God that you are prepared to receive.

"Cleanliness is next to godliness" is more than a cliché. It speaks to the purity of spirit that comes from a life well-tended. God is holy. He inhabits clarity, peace, and structure.

Order begins with intention. Moving forward is the foundation. Commit to honoring what you have. Your body is a temple. Your home is a sanctuary. Your mind is a garden. What you do with these gifts reveals how seriously you take the life God has given you.

Self-care is awareness—it is stewardship. It is tending to the temple of your being. A rested body, a nourished soul, a quiet mind—these are spiritual necessities.

When you prepare your meals with mindfulness, when you declutter your space, when you rest with purpose, you are honoring God by honoring what He created. This is worship in motion. It's gratitude with hands and feet.

We see examples in Jesus' ministry where He retreated to quiet places. He stepped away from the crowd to pray, to rest, to realign. If the Son of God needed to find solitude, so do we.

In Matthew 25:14–30, Jesus tells the parable of a master who entrusted his servants with talents (a form of currency). Two servants invested and multiplied what they were given. One buried his gift in fear. The master called that servant wicked and lazy—not because he failed to double the money, but because of fear.

God is looking for faithfulness. Order is a sign of stewardship. When you care for what you've been given, God knows He can trust you with more.

Disorder is spiritual, mental, emotional, and physical. Some of us are emotionally cluttered. Our thoughts are tangled with worry, our hearts knotted with past pain, our spirits weighed down by unforgiveness.

Doubt, fear, and worry are emotions as well as spiritual blocks. They clog the channels through which divine wisdom flows. But when we surrender these things to God, when we choose peace over panic, clarity comes. Peace is order in motion.

"You will keep in perfect peace those whose minds are steadfast, because they trust in You." —Isaiah 26:3

Judging others disrupts our own peace. It consumes our focus. It shifts our energy away from healing and toward division. Judgment is a form of spiritual clutter. It tangles our minds in bitterness and distraction.

"Do not judge, or you too will be judged. For in the same way you judge others, you will be judged, and with the measure you use, it will be measured to you." —Matthew 7:1–2

Instead of pointing fingers, turn inward. Examine your own heart. Ask: What am I avoiding? What am I afraid to confront in myself?

This world is filled with energies, spirits, and influences. Not all of them are for your good. That's why you must guard your gates. What you watch, what you listen to, who you allow into your space—all of it matters.

Discernment is spiritual protection. It helps you identify what aligns with your calling and what pulls you away. Think of discernment as spiritual PPE—personal protective equipment for your soul.

Psalm 1 warns us of the progression of spiritual compromise:

"Blessed is the man who does not walk in counsel of the wicked, or stand in the way of sinners, or sit in the seat of mockers."

To walk is to entertain. To stand is to engage. To sit is to be comfortable.

Avoid environments that dull your spirit and dilute your purpose. Choose community that lifts you. Choose words that build. Choose habits that reflect the fruit of the Spirit.

Words are seeds. Every sentence you speak plants something in the atmosphere. Will it be peace or conflict? Healing or harm?

Gossip is spiritual poison. It may taste sweet to the tongue, but it sours the soul. Speak only what is true, and edifying. Be slow to speak, quick to listen, slow to anger (James 1:19).

Order can be rigid, more importantly it is rhythmic. It is intentional flow. It is waking up with purpose and going to sleep with peace. It is letting go of what no longer serves you. It is decluttering your space, your heart, and your spirit. It is saying, "I trust God enough to bring my life into alignment with His will."

Let your daily routines become rituals of reverence. Let your home be a haven of peace. Let your mind be a sanctuary of clarity.

Let your life be a living sacrifice—holy, intentional, pleasing to God.

Chapter 8: Talents

The Parable of the Talents (Matthew 25:14–30) is a powerful spiritual lesson wrapped in a simple story. It begins with a master preparing for a long journey. Before departing, he entrusts his servants with his wealth: to one, he gives five talents; to another, two; and to the last, one. Each amount is distributed according to the servant's ability. This detail is crucial. God gives us what we can handle to invite us into faithfulness.

The servant given five talents went to work immediately. He traded, invested, and doubled his portion. The one with two talents doubled also. But the servant with one talent did something very different. Driven by fear, he buried his gift. He hid it in the earth, untouched and unused.

When the master returned, he asked for an account. The first two stepped forward joyfully, showing the fruit of their labor. The master rewarded them both for their faithfulness.

"Well done, good and faithful servant! You have been faithful with a few things; I will put you in charge of many. Come and share in your master's happiness."

But the servant who had buried his one talent came forward full of excuses. He projected fear and blame, saying, "Master, I knew you to be a hard man...so I was afraid. I hid your gold. Here it is."

And the master replied:

"You wicked and lazy servant! If you knew that I reap where I have not sown, why didn't you at least deposit my money with the bankers, so I could have received it back with interest?"

The servant's talent was taken and given to the one with ten, and he was cast into outer darkness.

This parable is about more than gold—it's about purpose, responsibility, and accountability. The talents represent all that God has entrusted to you: your gifts, resources, time, ideas, relationships, opportunities, health, voice, and breath.

To bury your talent is to withhold your purpose. It's to disconnect from your divine assignment. You may not squander it in obvious ways, but doing nothing is also a decision. It is spiritual negligence.

God doesn't expect perfection—He expects movement. Faithfulness. Risk. Courage. Your gifts are meant to be multiplied, not hidden. Fear is not an option! They were given to bless the world, to advance the Kingdom, and to deepen your relationship with the Giver.

If you're waiting for the "perfect time" to start using your gifts, there is no better time than the present. The perfect time is now. God calls the willing, not the flawless. He perfects what we give Him.

Greatness can be found with one talent. Your gifts intertwined with your strength and purpose are needed for the greatest impact. You need only to be faithful with your portion.

The servant's downfall was not that he failed, but that he feared. Fear led to paralysis. It justified inaction. But in the Kingdom of God, fear is not an excuse, it is unacceptable.

Multiplication is financial, material, and spiritual. When you operate in your gifts, they multiply. Your peace multiplies. Your joy multiplies. Your impact multiplies.

God's economy works through stewardship. When you use what you have with intention, it grows. When you hold on to it in fear, it withers.

The servant cast into darkness represents the soul that disconnects from purpose. Poverty of the spirit is worse than poverty of possessions. You can have wealth and still be barren. You can have little and still be rich in joy, love, and purpose.

The Kingdom of Heaven is not about appearance; it's about alignment. Are you aligned with what God has placed in you?

God placed something divine inside you. And He is coming back to see what you did with it.

Ask yourself: Have I buried anything? Has fear silenced my gift? Have I convinced myself that what I have isn't enough?

Dig it up. Dust it off. Begin again.

Reflection Practice: Unveiling Your Talents

Find a quiet space and reflect deeply:

What has God placed in your hands?

Write down your gifts, passions, strengths, and opportunities.

Have you buried anything out of fear, shame, or insecurity?

Be honest. Name what you have hidden.

What is one small action you can take this week to use your talent?

It might be a conversation, a creative step, an act of service.

Who might benefit from your obedience?

Think about the ripple effect of showing up fully.

Write a prayer of recommitment:

Offer your talents back to God. Ask Him to breathe on them.

Affirmation:

I am not afraid. I will not bury what God has entrusted to me. I will walk in faith, multiply my gifts, and share in my Master's joy. My life will be fruitful, and my gifts will serve others. I was created for such a time as this.

Let this be the chapter where you return to what you buried. Let this be the moment your faith gets activated and your talents come alive.

Because when you do, Heaven rejoices. And your Master will say, "Well done."

Chapter 9: Forgiveness is the Transformation

"Do not conform to the pattern of this world, but be transformed by the renewing of your mind..." — Romans 12:2

Transformation is a spiritual process. It begins the moment you start believing—truly believing. Belief is the first step. Belief in life after death. Belief in the eternal soul. Belief in the divine power God has placed inside of you.

You were purposefully made. Within you lives the very breath of God, and with that breath comes purpose, destiny, and the invitation to walk in the light.

When that belief takes root, life begins to shift. You stop reacting, and you begin responding with purpose. This is the turning point from wandering to walking in destiny.

True transformation cannot happen in isolation. Spiritual growth flows in two directions:

Vertically—your relationship with God.

Horizontally—your relationship with others.

The deeper your intimacy with God, the more your life will radiate patience, love, and grace toward others. And the more you practice compassion and presence with those around you, the more attuned you become to the heartbeat of God.

Jesus said, "Love the Lord your God with all your heart... and love your neighbor as yourself" (Matthew 22:37–39). This is the spiritual blueprint for transformation.

Spiritual maturity is not measured by the number of scriptures you know or the hours spent in solitude. It's seen in how you show up for others. How you speak, listen, forgive, serve, and honor people—especially when it's inconvenient, uncomfortable, or undeserved.

Be someone others can count on. Show up with compassion. Show up with presence. Sometimes, the most powerful gift you can offer is your silent solidarity.

Empathy is not pity. It is entering into another's pain without needing to escape it or explain it. It's saying, "I'm here. You are not alone."

Even love, when misapplied, can become abusive. Sometimes, what we call "helping" is really control. Advice not rooted in discernment can wound more than it heals. That's why we must walk in the Spirit.

"There is a time to be silent and a time to speak." (Ecclesiastes 3:7)

Love without wisdom can become manipulation. Listen for the Spirit before you speak. There is power in restraint. The Savior's position has already been filled. Your assignment is to love. To reflect God's character.

God does not barge in. He invites. He knocks. He waits. In the same way, we must walk with open hands honoring each soul's sacred timeline.

This is how transformation becomes sustainable: when it flows from love, not fear; from grace, not ego.

If transformation is a journey, then forgiveness is the gate you must pass through again and again.

Forgiveness is freedom. Holding on to grudges, hatred, and unresolved conflict is like chaining yourself to the very person or pain you wish to escape. That chain becomes a prison for you. Forgiveness does not mean forgetting or excusing wrongs; it means releasing the power of that wrong to dominate your life.

If possible, make amends. Go to those you have wronged. Apologize sincerely. Give back what was taken, whether it was time, peace, love, or even material things. This is not weakness—it is strength. Owe no one anything.

Debt is a pitfall. It is a shadow that creeps into the mind at night, strangling peace and causing fear and anxiety. It leads people into desperation—forcing some into soul-draining jobs or dark paths they were never meant to walk. Avoid debt when you can. It is a form of bondage. Ask for wisdom and stewardship, and God will guide your steps.

Forgiveness is not forgetting. It is not pretending you weren't hurt. Forgiveness is saying: This pain no longer has permission to control me.

Forgiveness must be extended to yourself. For the things you didn't know. For the ways you survived. For the bridges burned, and the time lost. Extend grace inward—because your soul cannot thrive in shame.

Walk wisely. Align your finances, your time, your energy with Heaven's priorities. Freedom is your birthright in Christ today.

Transformation is not linear. There are days when you will soar and days when you will crawl. There will be moments of clarity and moments of doubt. Growth is not perfection, it's persistence.

Mistakes will happen, there will be roadblocks—they are teachers. Learn, adjust, keep moving. Don't build your identity around your wounds.

You are becoming.

Let your emotions pass through you, not control you. Observe your anger. Acknowledge your grief. Process your fear. But do not let them take the throne of your heart. Only God belongs there.

Jesus said, "Let the dead bury their own dead" (Luke 9:60). Not as a dismissal of grief, but as a reminder: You are called to life. You are called to rise.

There is a time to grieve, to reflect, and to learn—but we are not meant to live in the valley of sorrow and failure. Staying too long in that low place weakens the spirit and clouds your vision.

Resurrection power lives in you. You are here to grow, to bloom, to multiply. Do not worship what has died. Honor it. Grieve it. Then rise from it.

Reflection Questions:

What part of your life is calling for transformation today?

Where do you need to release control and allow the Spirit to lead?

Who are you being called to forgive—yourself included?

Are there areas in your life where you're offering help from ego instead of love?

How can you practice love with wisdom and boundaries this week?

You are on a sacred journey. And it is not easy—but it is worth it. With every step you take in faith, Heaven moves with you. With every small act of obedience, transformation unfolds.

Let the old fall away. Let the new emerge. Let the Spirit breathe through you until every corner of your life shines with the truth: You are chosen. You are growing.

Keep walking. The transformation is just beginning.

Chapter 10: Healing of the Heart

Often, it's easy to love a neighbor, it's another to love an enemy. A neighbor might annoy you, inconvenience you, or differ from you. But an enemy? An enemy attempts to harm you. An enemy will betray you. An enemy threatens your safety, emasculates your dignity, and disturbs your peace. To love such a person—someone who has wronged you or someone you love—can feel not just unnatural, but offensive to our sense of justice. And yet, that is exactly where divine love begins.

"Love your neighbor as yourself," Jesus taught, summing up the entire law and the prophets in one instruction. "But I tell you, love your enemies and pray for those who persecute you." These words, recorded in Matthew's Gospel are a spiritual guide. They are radical, earth-shaking truths meant to unchain us from bitterness, vengeance, and the prisons we build within our own hearts.

Love is the highest force in the universe. Love is power. It is the force that carried Christ through betrayal, torture, and death—love that looked at His murderers and said, "Father, forgive them, for they know not what they do." It is the glue that holds all things together. It is the breath that hovered over the waters in the beginning and the Word that became flesh. It is the essence of God Himself, for God is not a being with love—He is love.

To love is not to excuse evil, but to transcend it. To love is to resist the pull of retaliation and choose the higher way. To love is to defy the gravitational weight of offense and rise into freedom. When you love in the face of hatred you claim your power. For hatred is a chain that binds both victim and aggressor. But love breaks chains.

This is why Scripture says, "Love never fails." It doesn't mean love always feels good, or that it always brings immediate resolution. But it means love never stops being effective. It leaves an imprint. It changes the atmosphere. It opens a door to redemption, even when no one walks through it. Love is the greatest eternal thing you can give or receive.

We often speak of love as a feeling, but it is far more than that. Feelings change. Love remains. Love is a decision, a discipline, a daily surrender. It is something you rise into. And every time you choose love over resentment, over sarcasm, over coldness, you rise. You begin to heal.

The human heart is more than a biological organ—it is an energetic center where the physical and spiritual realms converge. When the mind and heart are in coherence, a sacred alignment occurs—one that unlocks the flow of power and invites true healing to begin.

Science tells us the heart is electrical, generating the strongest electromagnetic field in the body, while the mind is magnetic, drawing in experiences and shaping perceptions. This mirrors divine design: the mind attracts, and the heart activates. It is in the heart where emotions live and where pain is felt deeply. The spiritual heart is the seat that connects to the source—the place where God writes His will, where the soul hears His voice, and where transformation begins. When your thoughts and emotions come into agreement with will, your entire being begins to resonate with purpose—and your life begins to move with divine power.

The heart is the seat of our will, our spirit, our affections. It's where faith is planted, or fear is watered. That's why Proverbs warns, "Above all else, guard your heart, for everything you do flows from it." Our time and our truth. Our image and our intimacy with God.

What happens when the heart is broken? What happens when life shatters it, when people wound it, when loss drains it dry? What happens when the heart grows cold, crusted with disappointment, suffocated by sorrow? How do we heal that which we barely understand ourselves?

We begin with the gifts that flow from God's Spirit: love, peace, joy, and laughter. These are holy tools.

Love, when poured into the wounded heart, begins to soften. It is the balm that seeps into the cracks created by rejection, betrayal, abandonment, and regret. Love sees what is and what could be. When we open even the smallest door to God's love, the process begins. Love whispers to the soul, "You are magnificent. You're worthy of redemption."

Stillness promotes healing and peace. Peace is the tangible presence of God in the middle of it all. Peace is what allowed Jesus to sleep in a boat tossed by waves. Peace is what guarded Paul in prison and sustained David in exile. It can change the external from within. When peace takes its place on the throne of the heart, anxiety has no seat. Worry must wait. You find yourself breathing deeper. Thinking clearer. Loving freer. Healing becomes possible when you stop fighting and start resting.

Then comes joy, it could be the buzz of a good day or a temporary win, it is most importantly the joy of the Lord. This joy is rooted in something deeper than circumstance. It flows from knowing who you are and whose you are. It rises from the well of gratitude. It dances even in drought. This joy can be found in adverse situations. It says, "God is still good, even here." And in that confession, the soul finds its footing.

Healing can come through tears, prayer, and laughter. Yes, laughter. A holy medicine prescribed by The Creator. Scripture says: A joyful heart is good medicine," and "a time to weep and a time to laugh, a time to mourn and a time to dance."

Laughter reminds us that sorrow is temporary. When you laugh, the child in you wakes up—the part that remembers Eden, that remembers joy without guilt, freedom without fear. When you laugh, through pain, you make a prophetic declaration: "I am here. I will not be crushed. There is something to celebrate."

Laugh with others. Laugh at yourself. Laugh with God. Let your laughter be an act of defiance against despair, a song of rebellion against bitterness. When you do, healing can flow, for love is greater.

To heal the heart is to allow God to transform your pain into purpose. It is to bring the ashes of your story to the altar and let The Creator exchange them for beauty. Healing manifests when the past no longer controls the present. It means you are free to feel again. Free to dream again. Free to love again.

Healing takes time. It takes intention. It takes surrender. It requires you to choose vulnerability over vengeance, and faith over fear. It asks you to lay down your armor and let the hands of God touch the places you've kept hidden. You must choose it daily. In how you speak. In what you replay in your mind. In what you hold onto—and what you let go.

Begin with gratitude. Thank God for what you survived, even if you don't yet understand it. Open your heart. Let love pour in. Let peace wash over you. Let joy rise up. And let laughter fill the spaces once filled with pain.

When your heart returns home to God, when your inner being aligns again with love, the cracks don't disappear—they become windows. The scars don't vanish—they become stories. And in that wholeness, you survive, you shine. You become a light for others. A living testimony.

In the hands of the Creator, your heart is safe. In His presence, your healing is possible and it's inevitable.

And in His love, you will be made whole.

Chapter 11: Words, Prayers, and Affirmations

In the beginning, in the stillness there was a void of shape, breath, movement—Spirit hovering over the deep. Then came the Word. A declaration. "Let there be light," God said—and the darkness surrendered. With one spoken command, creation ignited. Galaxies spiraled into being. Oceans formed. Light exploded across the void.

Everything began with a Word.

The universe began with a word and that blueprint still holds true. You, fashioned in the image of a speaking God, carry the power. You were made to reflect His love and bear His likeness—you were made to echo His voice. Your words carry weight. They are seeds. They are weapons. They are doors.

"Death and life are in the power of the tongue," Proverbs reminds us. We often recite that verse as a warning, however it is a promise. You are powerful in the shaping of your destiny. Your tongue is a brush, and your words are the strokes that paint the future. Every sentence you speak is either reinforcing a chain or loosening one. You are either reinforcing a prison or building a palace. And if God created the heavens with a Word, what might your words create?

Be careful, then, with the way you speak about yourself. You are listening. Your spirit is always listening. Don't curse yourself with careless confessions like "I'm always anxious," or "Nothing good ever happens to me," or "I guess I'll never change." These phrases may seem small, but they are spiritually loaded. They plant themselves in the garden of your soul and take root. What begins as sarcasm or frustration can grow into self-fulfilling prophecy if you are not vigilant.

Declare what you hope for. Declare what is true, even when your feelings haven't caught up to it. Speak what God has promised. Speak life into your home. Speak blessings over your body. Speak healing over your heart. Speak truth into your thoughts. Speak destiny over your children. Speak purpose into your every step.

Words are communication and they are creation. Prayer can be a wish and also a weapon. Praise is spiritual warfare. The vibrations of your voice carry power in the unseen realm. It breaks strongholds. It plants seeds. It sends ripples through dimensions you cannot see but are deeply connected to. Whether in a whispered prayer, a joyful song, or a silent chant rising from the depth of your soul, your voice is a force.

The earth responds to sound. Mountains move at His command. Demons tremble at His name. Heaven listens when you speak in faith. Your words, when aligned with truth, become spiritual commands that heaven honors.

"Speak the truth, and the truth will set you free." It should be spoken. It should be believed internally but declared externally.

This is the foundation of true manifestation, the biblical principle of fulfillment. What you speak matters. Manifestation is not magic; it is alignment. It follows divine principles, much like planting a seed.

First, you must choose the right seed—your intention, your vision. Next, you must plant that seed at the appointed time, in fertile soil—your belief, your preparation. Before anything ever breaks the surface, the seed responds to the soil. It germinates. It grows roots in darkness. It becomes before it is seen. Don't give up before the sprout appears—the seed is the miracle. To truly know yourself, you must understand this: you are the miracle.

As it is written in Matthew 17:20:"If you have faith as small as a mustard seed, you can say to this mountain, 'Move from here to there,' and it will move. Nothing will be impossible for you."

To manifest is to awaken—to begin a journey of becoming. It is to walk in the Spirit of God as a seeker, a traveler in tune with the Creator of all things. From faith to faith. From seed to harvest. From vision to reality.

Submit yourself to the process. Endurance must have its full work. When it occurs, you will be complete, lacking nothing.

You will stumble. Mistakes are the curriculum of growth. Every misstep teaches. Every lesson learned becomes wisdom. Do not dwell in the valley of sorrow and failure. The soul and the spirit are not concerned with your embarrassment or the opinions of others. That is the voice of the ego. Separate yourself from it.

Observe the emotions that rise after you fall. Contain them. Study them. Don't confuse them with who you are.

Planting begins with intention. You must first ask yourself: What am I truly sowing? What vision am I nurturing with my thoughts and declarations? What future am I preparing for with my inner dialogue? If your words are seeds, then your daily speech is shaping your harvest.

Some seeds come from hope. Others from fear. Some from Godly principles. Others from fleshly ego. Discernment is crucial. Not every desire is righteous. Not every longing is aligned. That's why intimacy with God is essential, to ensure you are not planting what you want, but what He has willed. Ask Him to refine your desires. Then declare with boldness the promises He confirms.

Every seed needs soil. Your inner world, the condition of your heart, the environment of your daily life, is the soil where that seed either grows or dies. Bitterness, distraction, fear, gossip, and cynicism are toxic terrain. On the other hand, gratitude, discipline, community, truth, and faith? That is fertile ground. When your soil is healthy, your seed has a chance to break through.

Even the most powerful seed, planted in the richest soil, still requires patience. There will be seasons when it feels like your prayers are unheard, your affirmations are empty, and your faith is futile. But that is the precise moment when faith becomes real. In the silence before the bloom.

Jesus said that faith the size of a mustard seed can move mountains. Why? A sentence of truth spoken in trembling faith can open the gates of heaven.

Say the prayer. Sing the song. Chant the promise. Praise in the hallway before the door opens. Affirm what God has said, even when doubt howls back. Do not grow weary. Do not stop watering your seeds with faith. Your words are working. Your prayers are plowing. Your praise is preparing the ground for miracles.

Speak light into darkness. Speak growth into stagnation. Speak healing into pain. Speak abundance into lack. Speak peace into chaos. Speak love into fear.

You are a vessel of Godly vibration. Your voice is a tool. Your faith is the soil. Your life is the harvest.

The same Word that spoke light into being, that split seas, that raised the dead, that Word now lives in you. Through whisper, through declaration, through breath of belief, the creative power of the beginning continues through your very being.

Chapter 12: Hell Is Real

It is a real destination, a realm of consequence, and a spiritual condition that begins long before death. The Bible references hell more than 25 times, describing it as a place of torment, weeping, utter darkness, and complete separation from God. It is the manifestation of divine justice, a response in creation, a God who cannot coexist with sin and unrepentant rebellion.

Hell was not created for man, it was created for demons. Scripture is clear: "He is patient with you, not wanting anyone to perish, but everyone to come to repentance." (2 Peter 3:9) Yet, God will not force Himself on you. Love does not manipulate. Grace must be accepted. Mercy must be received. When people reject the invitation to walk in light, they remain in darkness—and hell is the final consequence of that chosen separation.

Jesus spoke of hell often. In Matthew 10:28, He warned, "Do not fear those who kill the body but cannot kill the soul. Rather, be afraid of the One who can destroy both soul and body in hell." The Creator of life is a righteous Judge.

Hell is described as Gehenna, a burning valley used as a trash heap outside Jerusalem, a place of decay and destruction. In spiritual terms, it represents more than fire. It is spiritual isolation. It is the soul's experience of being fully cut off from the presence, peace, and person of God. Where heaven is relationship, hell is disconnection. Where heaven is wholeness, hell is torment. Where heaven is light, hell is darkness.

Hell is not reserved for the recognizably wicked. It is for those who lived indifferent to truth. For those who buried their talents. For those who hurt the innocent and never repented. For those who worshiped self and served their appetites, never acknowledging the Creator who gave them breath. Hell is not solely for murderers and thieves. It is for those who refused the invitation of grace.

Justice requires payment. Every soul matters to God. The cries of abused children, the tears of the oppressed, the agony of those unjustly harmed, nothing escapes God's eye. "Shall not the Judge of all the earth do what is just?" (Genesis 18:25) Hell is justice for the evil done to the innocent, for every debt not paid on this side of eternity. It is not vengeance; it is accountability.

"Do not be deceived: God is not mocked. A man reaps what he sows." (Galatians 6:7)

This is the spiritual law of sowing and reaping. What you sow in thought, word, and deed, you will reap. Heaven and hell are future realities. They are present experiences. You begin to taste them now, based on how you live. Choose peace, truth, mercy, and love, you begin to taste heaven. Choose hatred, anger, deceit, greed, and unforgiveness and you begin to breathe the fumes of hell. The soul feels it. The body carries it. Depression, anxiety, anger, rage, many of these burdens are spiritual symptoms of separation from The Creator. They are signals. They are the soul's way of crying out for reconnection with the Divine.

The good news? You can change today. Right now. Repentance is the bridge from darkness to light. Grace must be accepted. Salvation is received.

Yeshua endured separation so that we would never have to. On the cross, He cried out, "My God, My God, why have You forsaken Me?" (Matthew 27:46). In that moment, He bore the full weight of our sin and tasted the separation that defines hell. He went to the depths so we wouldn't have to. But if we reject this gift, we choose to stand alone.

No one stumbles into hell. It is a slow and steady series of choices, a refusal to surrender, an insistence on self-lordship. It is the consequence of a heart hardened against light. But you, beloved, were made for heaven. You were designed for communion, joy, and freedom.

Hell is real as is Heaven.

Let your thoughts rise like incense, your choices flow like rivers of righteousness, and your heartbeat echo the rhythm of heaven. Let each moment reflect your eternal path. Choose life, truth, and God.

Reflection Exercise: Awakening to Eternity

How do your daily choices reflect your spiritual destination?

Have you been avoiding change out of fear or pride?

What does justice mean to you, and how does God's justice bring peace to your understanding of eternity?

Is there an area of your life where you are living in separation from God?

Write a prayer of surrender and recommitment. Invite God to restore, heal, and lead you into life.

Affirmation: I was not created for darkness, I was created for light. I walk in truth, I accept grace, and I choose the presence of God, now and forever.

Chapter 13: Subdue It

"And God blessed them, and God said unto them, be fruitful, and multiply, and replenish the earth, and subdue it...'" — Genesis 1:28

"And as for you, be fruitful and multiply; increase greatly on the earth and multiply in it." — Genesis 9:7

Before any law was written, before any commandment was chiseled into stone, there was a word spoken directly from the mouth of God to humankind: Be fruitful, multiply, fill, subdue, and have dominion.

In these early verses of Genesis, we find more than poetic origin stories; we find marching orders. And within those orders is a framework for how to live a life of purpose and productivity.

To be fruitful is to be a light and be connected to the divine. It is exponential growth in impact, and in faith. To multiply is to produce. To bear results. To yield something meaningful from your life.

God provided a mandate to replenish the earth and subdue it. We are called to take up spiritual, emotional, physical, and mental space in the world with boldness, without hiding or minimizing who we are, to fully show up and live out our purpose.

To subdue is to influence, by intention, by creativity, and by the power of manifestation. To have dominion is to rule. To be responsible for what God has given you. To be a steward of your gifts, your time, your family, your calling, and your failures. This is about transforming it.

Subduing is to bring under discipline, to gain mastery. If you can master your hands, you can become a Leonardo Davinci. If you can master the basketball, you can become a Stephen Curry. If you can master your mind, you can unlock the genius within. You subdue when you keep showing up, when you practice until your talent becomes skill.

Subduing can be forceful and is shaped with focus. It is the act of turning potential into power through intentional practice.

Many believers ask, "What is my purpose?" But in Genesis 1:28 and reiterated in Genesis 9:7, God gave us a universal purpose. Before you were a writer, parent, teacher, or entrepreneur, you were called to produce life biologically, spiritually and creatively.

To "multiply" includes breathing life into dreams, stewarding ideas, growing character, and developing the talents that reflect God's image in you.

To be fruitful and multiply is to leave an inheritance for your children's children. What you plant should become a tree. What you learn should be passed on. What you do should produce disciples.

God's command was to first subdue, before you reign over something, you must shape it. Mold it. Confront it. Develop it.

When He told Adam and Eve to "be fruitful and multiply," they were capable of producing life. When He said to subdue, they were endowed with childbearing, tending the land and flocks, physical strength, and spiritual insight.

The implication of Genesis 1:28 and 9:7 are: We are called to populate the earth with people and to populate it with light.

Your ideas are light. Your compassion is light. Your integrity in business is light. Your forgiveness in relationships is light.

Children raised in love and truth are carriers of light. Books written from divine insight are containers of light. Businesses founded on integrity are systems of light.

This is what it means to be fruitful: increasing the presence of God's goodness in every sphere of you life.

You were born to thrive. To fill the world with something eternal. Your obedience becomes light. Your purpose becomes legacy. Your manifestation becomes worship and admiration.

Don't miss this: Everything God directed us to do, be fruitful, multiply, fill the earth, subdue it, and have dominion requires attention, focus and guidance. Whereas fruitfulness requires sowing in seasons of drought. Filling the earth requires moving out of comfort zones. Subduing requires confronting chaos. Dominion requires maturity and wisdom.

We serve a God who empowers becoming. In Genesis 1:28, God instructs us—He is revealing who we are to become.

Fruitful. Multipliers. Manifestors. Subduers. Kings and queens with dominion.

These are our responsibilities. You are building a life; you are shaping reality with God's breath inside of you. And the world benefits your becoming.

So how do we walk in this Genesis mandate today?

Here are five practical ways to live fruitfully and manifest your divine dominion:

Plant Seeds Daily Speak life. Take action. Write the chapter. Make the call. Apologize. Apply. Don't underestimate the small acts—they add up. Every great tree began as a seed.

Commit to Multiplication What you know, teach. What you build, replicate. What you overcome, share. Multiply the goodness in your life by refusing to hoard it.

Fill the Room With Purpose Whether it's your home, your job, your community, or your social media—fill the space you inhabit with something meaningful. You are the light.

Subdue Through Practice Don't run from the blank canvas, the empty stage, the new season. Practice until it bends. Subdue it by staying faithful and don't faint.

Take Dominion With Grace Lead with humility. Influence with empathy. Own your calling with reverence. This is not about ego—it's about love.

The words in Genesis were intentional. They were for then and they are for now. You were created with a purpose that echoes through the very first breath God breathed into humankind. You are the fulfillment of a divine pattern. You are the evidence of a spiritual design. And you are being called—to manifest.

You were made from the earth and you were made for it.

Chapter 14: Who Are You

"Before I formed you in the womb I knew you, before you were born I set you apart." —Jeremiah 1:5

Ask a person, 'Who are you?' and most will answer with what they do: I'm a teacher. I'm a mother. I'm a business owner. I'm a student. I'm an artist. However none of these are who they are. These are roles. Hats they wear. Chapters in their story. So, who are you, really?

The truth is, most of us haven't been taught how to answer that question. We live in a culture that prizes productivity, the caste system, labels, and identity by function. But God defines identity by function and by essence—both by being and doing. This chapter is about peeling back every label, title, and performance metric. It's about returning to the truth of your identity: the part of you that existed before the world called you anything at all.

From the time we are children, we are encouraged to define ourselves by performance: - What do you want to be when you grow up? - What are you good at? - How do others see you? Included in spiritual spaces, we carry this mindset: 'I'm a servant of God,' 'I'm a worship leader,' 'I'm called to ministry.' While these can be true expressions of calling, they are still not the essence of who you are. Consider this: if every role in your life disappeared—if you lost your job, your title, your family roles, even your talents—who would you be? The work of this chapter is to unearth the core of your being, the you God created before you ever took your first breath. You are a three-part being: Spirit: The eternal part of you. The divine spark that communicates with God. Soul: Your heart, mind, will, and emotions—your personality and psychological experience.

Body: Your physical form, the vessel you inhabit on Earth.

Many people confuse their identity with their actions or traits. They might say, "This is who I am—I'm passionate, intelligent, driven, emotional, or logical." But these are expressions of your nature, not the core of who you are. Even more people mistake their mind's choices for destiny—choosing careers, paths, and relationships based purely on logic or societal pressure. But when your soul is misaligned with your spirit, you may succeed in the world and still feel unfulfilled. The soul is a powerful force, but it must submit to the spirit, because the spirit connects to God. And it is only in union with Him that you come into the truth of who you are.

When the prophet Samuel came to Jesse's house looking for the one God had chosen, no one expected it to be David. He was the youngest, out in the fields tending sheep, overlooked even by his own father. But God told Samuel:

"The Lord does not look at the things people look at. People look at the outward appearance, but the Lord looks at the heart." —1 Samuel 16:7

David had not yet slain Goliath. He had not yet led armies or written psalms. He had done nothing to prove himself as king. Yet God called him chosen. Beloved. Anointed.

That same truth is for you. You are not defined by what you achieve. You are not your title, your success, or your failures. You are chosen because God sees your heart, and He delights in you before you are even conscious.

You are a child of the Creator. You are known and loved. And from that identity, your life flows. One of the greatest tragedies is living out a life chosen by the mind alone. A job, a role, a lifestyle picked based on logic, pressure, or even ambition but not cosigned by God. "Unless the Lord builds the house, the builders labor in vain." —Psalm 127:1 When your mind alone picks your path, the house looks good from the outside, but the foundation is faulty. You may have the title, the accolades, the paychecks but you'll wrestle with discontent, fatigue, or an ache that no success can fill. Why? Because it wasn't blessed. God isn't punishing you it's because God blesses what is in alignment with your original design. When the soul is in submission to the spirit and the spirit submits to God something beautiful happens. Your soul begins to choose what God has already chosen for you. And now, what you do becomes a reflection of who you are. For example: - If your spirit resonates with healing, you may become a doctor because healing flows from your core identity. - If your spirit is drawn to beauty and order, you may be a designer because your soul delights in mirroring the creativity of God. - If your spirit is passionate about justice, you may become a lawyer because advocacy is part of your divine makeup. When your soul chooses a path in alignment with your spirit, the work becomes worship. Your job then can be part of who you are. But only when it flows from your essence, not from your ego. Here are some questions to help you return to your God-given essence: 1. Who were you before the world told you who to be? 2. What makes your spirit feel alive? 3. Where do you feel most connected to God? 4. If everything external were stripped away, what would remain? 5. What breaks your heart or stirs your compassion deeply? 6. When have you felt God's "yes" in your spirit? Let your answers speak not from your intellect, but from your innermost being.

Write them down. Pray over them. Ask the Spirit to reveal.

"For we are his workmanship, created in Christ Jesus for good works, which God prepared in advance for us to do."—Ephesians 2:10 You are a masterpiece. Before you are a worker, parent, spouse, or servant, you are a soul, chosen and loved, known and seen. As you live from that place, your life becomes abundant. To stay aligned with who you truly are, practice: - Stillness: Regularly quiet the noise so you can hear the spirit. - Discernment: When making decisions, ask: "Is this in alignment with my spirit and God's will?" - Integrity: Let your choices reflect your true values, it's not convenience or conformity. - Community: Surround yourself with people who see the real you and call you deeper. - Devotion: Spend time in the Word to let God remind you of who you are in Him.

Your trauma, your triumphs, or your titles don't make you who you are. You are a spirit, chosen by God, formed in love, created to express heaven on Earth in a way only you can. When you live from your essence you begin to flow. When your soul submits to your spirit, and your spirit submits to God, life becomes purpose-driven instead of pressure-filled. The question isn't "What do I do?" The real question is, "How do I become who God created me to be?" From there, you begin to align.

You were not created to fit into molds shaped by fear, culture, or comparison. You were made in the image of God—not to copy someone else's life, but to reflect the unique expression of God within you. When you stop chasing definitions from the world, you make space to be defined by the Word.

Let your identity be anchored in who God says you are. In the ordinary moments when no one is watching, when you're doing the dishes, when you're sitting in silence. That is where the soul finds its true posture, resting in God's truth rather than performing for affirmation.

So many live under false names—names like "Not Enough," "Too Much," "Broken," or "Unworthy." But the Creator calls you by a different name: "Beloved," "Chosen," "Redeemed," "Free." Your task is not to earn those names but to receive them.

Your purpose is a presence to be walked in. As you abide in Christ, your life will naturally bear fruit. You won't have to prove who you are; your very being will reveal it.

Take time to sit with God, without agenda or concern of the outcome. Ask Him to reveal how He sees you. Let His voice become louder than your inner critic, louder than your fears, louder than your past. His voice is the only one that knows your true name.

Remember, identity is not a destination—it's a revelation. It unfolds over time, deepens with prayer, and flourishes in surrender. And in each season, you are called to live both from the outside-in and from the inside-out.

Your spirit knows the truth. Your soul must agree with it. And your life will become an expression of it.

You are who God says you are. And that is more than enough.

Chapter 15: Tools for the Journey

Become aware—who is the captain of this ship? Your soul and spirit are your most valuable possessions. Cherish them.

To sleep is to be awake. To awaken is to sleep. While sleeping, the soul and spirit travel to and fro—they function as travelers of universes and participants in the forming of your reality.

Get plenty of sleep.

Solitude, prayer, fasting, and meditation are essential for creating a healthy environment for the soul and spirit. For the body temple: clean air, pure water, nourishing food, and movement are essential.

Maintain a healthy mind and body. Fasting: going without—with intention. It gives the soul and spirit space to reset, restore order, and regain divine control. Fast for clarity. Fast for deeper meditation. Fast for healing.

Movement: exercise, walking, stretching—is necessary for good health. It restores your connection with mind, body, soul, and spirit. Do it daily, intentionally, with gratitude.

Journaling is one of the most powerful tools you have. Forecasting: write down your goals before the day begins. And remember: the day begins in the evening.

Each evening, prepare your meals. Break your fast with what grows from the ground—fruits, vegetables, seeds, nuts, herbs. Eat them raw when possible and eat them alone. Let your food be healing.

Affirmations Before bed:

"I am prospering. I am healthy. I am wealthy. I walk with wisdom and discernment. I am a light in this universe."

In the morning, offer praise and thanksgiving. Declare affirmations out loud—affirm what is already done.

Get proper sunlight. Ground yourself whenever possible. Walk barefoot on the grass. Touch the earth. Breathe. Feel. Listen. Smell. Taste. See what God has done with your own senses. Reconnect with creation.

Work at least one hour each day toward your purpose. Work that's aligned with your calling should bring joy. If it doesn't, pause. Recalibrate. Ask God to show you where joy and purpose meet. Remember this: hard times happen even in purpose, being aligned will ensure you are on God's path.

Be holistic. Get outside. Nature stimulates the mind, body, soul, and spirit. Walk the beach. Embrace the wind. Admire the sky. This was all made for you.

Life is to be enjoyed. It is a gift. You were sent on purpose, with purpose to be a reflection of God on earth. You are a vessel of divine wisdom, a carrier of light, a living answer to someone's prayer.

Stand in that truth. Shine in that power.

Live because the kingdom of God is already within you. You are the miracle you've been waiting for.

Walk on water, heal the sick, and feed the poor.